I0412216

"As custodians of the planet it is our responsibility to deal with all the species with kindness, love and compassion. That these animals suffer through human cruelty is beyond understanding. Please help to stop this madness."

Richard Gere,
American Actor

BORN TO FLY

Published by Unison Communications Pty Ltd
Sydney Australia
Copyright ©1994, 2013 by Robyn Walker
robyn@unisoncommunications.com.au

ROBYN'S WEBSITES INCLUDE

www.BornToFly.com.au
Where you will find updated information on people and events related to animal rights plus her own postings and information on her next book in the 'Born to Fly' series.

www.UnisonCommunications.com.au
Robyn's team development & public events website

www.ConversationsWithRobyn.com
 Website for Robyn's first TV show, which featured conversations with Australian and international guests who are leaders in the areas of mind/body science, sustainability and spirituality.

www.ConversationsForABetterWorld.com.au
Website for the new TV show that Robyn is currently creating.

FOREWORD

'Born to Fly' is based on true-life stories of captive birds being safely released back into nature...blended with a fictional story about a Rainbow Lorikeet named Cherub. Although on one level it can be viewed as a children's book, it is predominantly a book for all ages, for storytelling and learning is universal.

Cherub was born in captivity and therefore did not understand that she was a bird who was put on the Earth to fly in the summer breezes and ride the thermal air streams. Cherub didn't even know what flying was, until taken from her mother and placed in a pet shop to be sold.

It was in the shop, among the other birds and animals that Cherub started to understand a little more of who she was. However it was not until she was sold, and one day had a Short Billed Corella fly down to her cage and talk with her, did she begin to understand her mother's last words.

As Cherub had been torn from the warmth of her mother's feathers, she heard her mother cry out 'Fly my child. You were born to experience the freedom of flight. When you get the chance to fly – let nothing stop you – fly and be free, for Cherub my child you were born to fly!'

And thus begins Cherub's self-education and life journey, to free other captive birds, and enlighten us all with her purity of heart and love for all creatures – two footed, four pawed, winged and finned.

It is a book based on valuing personal freedom and the underlying fact that as we imprison others we also imprison ourselves, and as we free ourselves, we automatically free others.

Philosophical – yes.
Metaphysical – yes.
Entertaining and educational – most definitely.

So although it may be seen as a children's book it is also geared towards adults – for there are levels within levels.

Was there a Rainbow Lorikeet named Cherub? – Yes.

And did she escape? – Yes, to fly free as was her natural birth right.

Where she flew though, only the Great Earth Mother knows.

DEDICATION

This book is dedicated to Squawky, the gallant Galah a Vet asked us to care for, with the hope we could nurture him back to health.

Unfortunately the permanent nerve damage to his cut wings; caused by an unknowing, unaware human to prevent Squawky from flying and escaping, resulted in so much ongoing pain, he continually self-mutilated.

Finally, along with the Vet, we made the heart breaking decision to end his physical pain, for good…and allow his earth bound spirit to finally fly free at last.

After we buried Squawky in the beautiful garden, I wrote this poem.

BORN TO FLY

You flew today

Your soul soared high,

Your wings

They moved with ease…

The sun shone bright

The sky beamed blue,

And Squawky

You flew

With the breeze

- 6.5.89 -

THE BIRTH OF CHERUB

Not long ago, in a small shed, a tiny life was born. As events go in our world, it was not seen as anything of much importance. In fact, no human was there to witness this beginning. The new mother shed a little tear for her newborn daughter, who she called Cherub.

Sadly for Cherub, she was born into a life of imprisonment, as was her mother and grandmother before her. She was born a captive -- with neither the dignity to fend for herself nor the freedom to come and go as she pleased.

She did not look her best either. Her eyes were closed; her limbs were floppy and unable to sustain her weight. Such was Cherub's lack of body covering, her mother sat huddled over her to keep her warm from the cold.

Unaware of her mother's great sadness and despair, Cherub slept on.

Suddenly, high above the small tin roof, a great white light was seen to appear.
A voice spoke softly to the mother. "Cry not mother. One day your daughter will be free. And she will bring love and freedom to many, and her name will be sung in the heavens."

Many wonderful things were told to the young mother that evening as the stars and moon shone down from the sky. When dawn heralded over the mountains, Cherub wriggled out from under her mother's warm coat, and she felt the sun's warm rays on her naked, unprotected skin.

Time passed...and Cherub grew strong from her mother's love and guidance. She loved waking up each day, snuggling next to her mother's soft downy feathers, and being fed from her mother's beak, for this is how mother birds feed their babies until they are old enough to feed themselves.

Cherub's own feathers began to grow and very soon she saw many wondrous colours emerging from her skin. She was astonished to see she was as pretty and colourful as her mother, who she thought was so beautiful to look at.

Cherub now had yellow, orange and green feathers of her own with a blue head and belly. She spent her days walking along the bottom of the cage, pecking at the grasses that grew wildly on the ground, or sitting next to her mother on the perch, gazing out through the wire of the cage and watching clouds roll by.

She was very happy being with her mother although often wondered why her mother seemed so sad at times, even though at other times she was so very happy and chirpy.

Soon however, people came to take Cherub away, and sell her into another form of captivity. To become the plaything, the possession of some man, woman or child who didn't understand you cannot truly buy or sell the freedom of another.

Cherub's mother cried tears of anguish yet again, only this time she shared the wise words with her daughter, that were told to her on the night of Cherub's birth.

"Although at this very moment in time you may not understand all that I am saying to you, in time you shall. Even though you were born in a cage and not with the touch of the breeze on your face, even though you have yet to spread your wings and feel the freedom you were born to, one day you shall. And one day someone will help provide you with the means to escape this life of bondage."

"When that day comes my child...seize the moment and do not hesitate. Fly my child; fly into the heavens to your freedom...and your destiny. For Cherub my daughter you were born to fly. That is your birthright and my gift to you. When you finally take it… let none take it back from you -- for you were born to experience the freedom of flight. You were **'Born to Fly!'**

THE PET SHOP

So how are all my lovelies this morning?' a woman's voice asked in joyful enthusiasm. Cherub realised it was Penny, who owned the pet shop.

Her words brought an initial hush over all the animals. Then, in the wink of an eye, the birds were once again chirping and chattering, the kittens meowed and purred, the puppies yapped and barked, the fish did another 'bloop' before swishing their tails and swimming past snails, which were sliding along the inside of the glass fish tanks.

The animals all acknowledged their approval of Penny's arrival. They knew she would now set about the task of feeding them, cleaning their cages and homes, and generally ensuring they were spick and span before being sold.

Jack, the white cockatoo, told Cherub all sorts of wonderful stories about being free and Jack knew what he was talking about. He was taken as an egg from his mother's nest, and hatched in an incubator. When Jack was old enough, he was placed in a very large and bushy aviary, helping to father more eggs.

Many years later, (cockatoos can live for a hundred years you know) Jack had outlived his usefulness and, rather than reward him by bonding him with a flock of wild cockatoos and setting him free, his owner gave him to Penny to try and sell. Jack had been in the same cage now for two years. It was so small he could only stretch one wing at a time. He was fearful that if ever he did have a chance to fly again, his wings may have seized up due to lack of exercise.

And then there was Bertie, a very old turtle who had lived happily in a large lake with his family. One day some men came and cut down trees near the lake to build a road. After they left, Bertie's curiosity got the better of him. He saw cars driving on the road so he went to have a look.

He slowly moved onto the road only to be hit by a fast sports car, which, even if he did see him, did not slow down, or try to avoid Bertie. It was very fortunate a young boy came along on his bike and saw his cracked shell. Luckily the boy's father was a vet and soon Bertie was as good as new. Unfortunately, the boy's father did not have enough room to keep Bertie, so off to the pet shop Bertie went.

Bertie really missed his family and was often upset to think that they may fear he was dead, or worse still, had deserted them. He was also worried that his children and grandchildren would go looking for him and without knowing about cars, could also be run over.

'And how are we all today?' a chirpy, high-pitched voice called out from somewhere near the ceiling. It was Sally Sparrow; she often flew in during the morning, picking at the seed that dropped from the bird's cages overnight. Penny had become so used to Sally that she allowed her to fly in and out of the shop as she wished.

Cherub found the sparrow an interesting friend, as Sally would tell all the animals the news for the day, like what was happening outside the shop, and sharing all her adventures with them.

Cherub still could not understand though why Sally was not in a cage.

Cherub did not understand that animals weren't born to be imprisoned. She had no idea that nature had meant for all animals to live freely, fulfilling their part in nature's own great tapestry of life, ensuring the perfect balance and harmony of all. Captivity was all she knew. She certainly did not understand that her fate was the cruelest of all because as a bird, nature had provided her with wings and therefore the freedom to fly anywhere she wished.

One day after school, a young girl came into the pet shop with her father and went straight to Cherub's cage.

'Daddy that's the one I saw the other day with mummy. It's the bird I want,' and before she knew it, Cherub was sitting in her new cage, on the back seat of a car, with the young girl by her side.

'Good luck little mate' were Jack's parting words to Cherub as she was taken from the shop. 'Remember the golden rule. If you get a chance to fly… fly quickly, fly high and fly free!'

CHERUB MEETS CORNY

Well one day rolled into the next for Cherub. She felt lonely at first because she missed all her friends from the pet shop. They had become her family after she was taken from her mother's gentle wings.

But she was happy enough. Her new cage hung outside under the roof of a back verandah and she was able to see all the trees in the garden. Sometimes other birds would fly into the trees to feed from the tree blossoms before flying off again. And when it rained, a small amount of water would find its way into Cherub's cage…if the breeze was blowing in the right direction. It was refreshing for her to have a chance to wash and cool down in the hot summer heat.

The people were nice also. The little girl fed Cherub with interesting flowers and leaves from the various trees and bushes in the garden. She also gave her fresh drinking water and seed each day, and tried very hard to speak with her and make friends.

Cherub though was becoming more and more lonely. She had never really been on her own before, without any birds or animals to talk with, and each day she looked out at the new dawn and wondered just why she was born. She had a vague memory of some words her mother said to her before she was taken away but they made no sense right now.

One sunny afternoon a bird flew from a tree and sat on her cage. 'Hello' said the bird, 'what's your name?' Cherub was so startled at first she thought she must have forgotten how to talk and the other bird started to fly off.

'Wait' cried Cherub.

'That's better' said the Corella, 'thought you must have been caged for so long that you were past saving.'
'What do you mean, 'past saving'?' asked Cherub.

'Well, you may have noticed some friends and me visiting the trees in the garden for some time now. We fly around searching for birds like you that are stuck in cages. We try to set them free. Trouble is, some birds have been caged on their own for so long, not only do they forget they can fly, they also forget they can talk. We can't really help them because if they can't talk with us then we're unable to teach them how to survive outside of captivity.'

Cherub didn't quite understand what this bird was saying but she knew that deep within her there was an excitement, an anticipation that she had never felt before. 'Who are you' she asked 'and what do you mean by 'set them free'?'

The Corella was startled by a noise coming from the house and quickly flew off into the wide expanse of blue sky, much to Cherub's disappointment.

Days went by and Cherub thought she must have been forgotten. Her little heart felt very confused and even lonelier now that she had talked and heard the strange words 'freedom' and 'fly' once more.

The long hot summer continued and Cherub became lost in a fever which one moment had her frying and another had her freezing. She knew if she could just have some water to immerse her whole body in she would be okay. She didn't know how she knew this, she just did.

'What do you think doc?' the father asked the vet.

'Well I'll give you some drops to put into her drinking water, and you really need to place a large bowl of water on the bottom of her cage so she can keep cool and clean herself. Birds in the wild can clean themselves naturally when it rains or cool themselves down in ponds and streams. Hopefully, if she survives the night, she'll be okay. And don't forget to change the water each morning so it doesn't become dirty and make her even more sick.'

The days went by and Cherub grew stronger. She had by now forgotten about the white Corella and so was quite startled when she heard a voice saying, 'you look a lot better.'
Cherub just stared and once again said nothing. 'Cat got your tongue?' the white Corella said, laughing hysterically.

'So, do you want to be set free?' he asked 'or do you want to hang around all day for the rest of your life'.
All Cherub could do was nod her head quickly and Corny, for that was his name, not just because he cracked corny jokes but because he also loved corncobs, told her what would happen.

'Now Cherub listen carefully' said Corny. 'Each day you must practise flapping your wings to build up the muscles. Ordinarily your mother would have taught you as a baby. She would then have pushed you out of the nest when she knew you were ready…and flown at your side as you tried your first wing flaps.'

'Practising may not seem easy at times however your wings are your freedom and therefore they must be strong and supple,' Corny continued.

The little girl was coming and Corny, flying off once more called out 'remember, practice flapping your wings…I'll be back.'

CHERUB FLIES FREE

Weeks passed and Cherub religiously practiced her wing flapping many times each day. The little girl noticed this and, one day as she was changing the water, asked her mother if she could take Cherub out of the cage. Her mother replied that if she did that, then the bird would probably fly away. 'The only way we can be sure she wouldn't escape is to cut her wings' she said.

That night Cherub could hear the little girl's parents discuss their daughter's request and it was decided that next morning they would cut Cherub's wings. Cherub heard all this and felt coldness deep within her chest and knew there was little she could do about it.

As the dawn rose, Cherub kept watch on the back door, feeling fear within her heart. Sure enough, the door opened and the little girl came running out, happy to think that at long last she could play with her birdie and have her sit on her shoulder.

The cage door opened and a large, hairy hand came in to grab her. Cherub squawked and backed off, trying to squeeze into the farthermost corner of her cage. 'You're scaring her,' said the mother, 'look at her little heart pumping in her chest.'

'Well what do you suggest I do?' asked the father.
'Let her settle down a bit while we have a think about it,' she replied.

They sat on the edge of the verandah looking at Cherub and discussing how best to tackle the problem.

Meanwhile, high in the trees, Corny and some of his mates were watching. They were also discussing their plan and just hoped they weren't too late to apply it. They knew that Cherub's wings would grow back, in time, and they could try again. However, sometimes two things could happen when a bird's wings were cut.

Firstly, sometimes the feathers were cut too close to the nerve endings of the wings and this could permanently deform a bird so it could never fly again and was very painful.

The other was that the longer a bird stayed in a cage, the more scared they were to fly free. They became so used to their little world that the thought of flying into the wide expanse of a blue sky, especially if they had never flown before, was too much for them, and they refused any help.

And then it happened!

The mother decided to try. As she put her hand in the cage, Cherub heard Corny squawking out urgently 'Hop onto her hand!. Hop onto her hand!'

Cherub started backing into the corner, afraid to do as Corny asked.

'Hop onto her hand!' Corny squawked out again. 'You're going to have to trust me. Please, hop onto her hand! I can't help you until you help yourself.' Such was the urgency in Corny's voice that Cherub, without thinking, did just that. She hopped onto the mother's hand.

Instantly Corny and two other Corellas flew down and buzzed around the woman's head, startling her. The mother was so taken aback that she immediately withdrew her hand from the cage...with Cherub standing on it!

'Quick!' Cherub heard Corny saying, 'Flap your wings as hard as you can and follow me. Hurry, hurry! Do it now! Do it now! Flap your wings now!'

Instinctively Cherub found herself flapping madly and, bit by bit, her whole body felt lighter as she went higher, and higher, and higher ...into the wide, open blue sky.
She was stunned!
She was flying!
Flying free...at long last!
Flying free and being herself...a bird!

It was then she heard her mother's voice from so long ago saying, '...seize the moment and do not hesitate! Then fly my child. Fly into the heavens to your freedom...and your destiny. For Cherub my child you were born to fly. That is your birthright and my gift to you. When you finally take it let no one take it back from you -- for you were born to experience the freedom of flight. You were **'Born to Fly!"**

CHERUB MEETS THE BALLINGER GANG

Months passed and Cherub grew stronger and more accustomed to being a bird.

She enjoyed the majesty of flying, soaring and riding the thermals, eating many types of berries and seeds; feeling the wind in her face and the rain on her feathers. Being with like-feathered friends and flying over large forests and enormous lakes. Oh she was so very happy she felt she could almost burst.

However there was one area in her life in which Cherub became sadder. Whenever she was flying around near houses, and saw birds, all sorts of birds, locked in their cages, her happiness for herself was replaced with despair for her fellow feathered friends.
How can I help you?' she asked Corny one day, when Corny was set to take off on one of his excursions to free more birds.

'I was wondering when you would ask me that' Corny replied with a lop-beaked smile. 'I think you're now strong enough to become one of our gang and to help us free more birds'.

Corny then introduced Cherub to Maxi Ballinger. Maxi was a long billed Corella and he shared his story with Cherub.

Maxi was also born into captivity, although unlike Cherub he had grown up in a very large bird aviary, so his mother taught him how to fly.

Like Cherub, Maxi too had been taken to Penny's pet shop and was bought by a woman called Lesley, when he was still a young bird. She hung his cage at the back of her verandah, which overlooked a beautiful garden with an enormously large, yellow, bloodwood tree that had lots of branches.

Maxi remembered the day he arrived.

Lesley shared a house with a friend called Christy. When Christy came home from work, she saw that Lesley had bought a Corella and hung it out the back in a cage. She and Lesley had a very big argument. Christy did not believe that birds should live in cages. She knew they were meant to fly as free as the wind.

It was not that Lesley was heartless, for it was she that named him Maxi Ballinger. Lesley had simply been brought up like many humans, seeing birds in cages and thinking that it must be okay.

And then one day, a few weeks later, Lesley was cleaning out Maxi's cage and Maxi simply snuck out. Lesley was very shocked and very upset, and also mystified as to how it actually happened. What she didn't know was that Maxi had been watching how she opened the cage door and, when she turned to get clean water for him, he opened it himself and flew out.

Lesley called out to Christy and together they ran around the neighbourhood with a ladder, hoping he would land on a tree and they could use the ladder to climb up and get him.

Although Christy did try to help Lesley, she was very happy that Maxi was now flying free and knew they would never recapture him. Eventually, Lesley came to know that also and they went home.

Lesley then built a bird platform in the back of the yard, placing water and seed on top for Maxi so he wouldn't go hungry. Lesley was a kind person and genuinely loved Maxi and wanted no harm to come to him.

Maxi eventually met up with two other long billed Corella's and together they began the Ballinger gang, flying around and helping captive birds escape from their cages.

Cherub listened in awe to Maxi's story.

'So now' said Maxi 'many birds of all kinds visit in the morning and afternoon at Lesley's backyard, as she always places seed and fresh water for us on the platform. Her garden is like a sanctuary for us and the trees she has planted have provided wonderful food from their blossoms and flowers.'

'In fact many of her friends come around in the afternoon and sit on her verandah simply to watch all the different bird species fly in to feed and catch up with what is happening in the bird world. The garden is really like a meeting place for all of us.'

'It is also here where we often find out from other feathered friends what new birds are around in cages for us to help free. It was Corny here who found you and came back to the yellow bloodwood tree to tell us. Would you like to join in our gang of freedom flying escapees and help us rescue and set free other captive birds?'

All Cherub could do was nod her head vigorously in reply as she was so moved by Maxi's story, and once again heard her mother's voice.

Corny then explained to Cherub, that the next day they were going to Lesley's house as a new bird had appeared in a cage on their back verandah. 'Apparently his name is Rocky.' The Ballinger gang had overheard Lesley and Christy the previous week talking about buying a caged short billed Corella from an advertisement they had seen in the local paper...and wondered why?

ROCKY AND SHORTY

Early next morning Cherub flew with Maxi, Corny and a number of other galahs, cockatoos and corellas to Lesley's house. This was her very first flight with the Ballinger gang and she was very excited.

'It's quite a meeting place' explained Corny as they flew in. 'Many species of bird congregate in the branches of the yellow bloodwood tree, flying down to the bird platform and feeding as they wish.'

Sometime later Cherub and the rest of the flock were chirping happily in the branches of the tree, watching Rocky in his cage.

'It's rather an interesting story' explained Shorty, another short-billed Corella who had been entrusted with this particular mission of getting to know Rocky, just as Corny had been selected to get to know Cherub when she was caged. Shorty too was an escapee and still bore the mark of what had been a ring around her left leg where she had been chained to a wooden rung so she couldn't fly off.

'Apparently Lesley bought Rocky from a place in the mountains and, from what we've heard; she intends to set him free'.

Cherub was astonished, as she had not heard of anyone willingly setting a bird they bought free.

Over the next month Cherub watched the gang fly down and sit on Rocky's cage, gradually getting to know him.

Rocky was very curious and listened closely to all that Shorty shared with him. Like Cherub, Rocky had also been born in captivity and had never really flown. Bit by bit though he began to practice flapping his wings. He also learnt from them what would happen once he flew free and how they would look after him.

Lesley and Christy would sit watching this picture unfold, hoping that the time would come when they felt sure enough that the other birds would look after Rocky.

As Rocky had been fed only seed in his previous home, the women began feeding him many different sorts of flowers and grasses. This was to help prepare him for when he was free. He would then know what sort of food to eat.

One of his favourites was Love Apples, a small red fruit that Lesley grew in big pots on her verandah.

And then the morning came when Lesley felt it was time to set Rocky free.

She placed the cage gently on the verandah, and carefully opened up the entire side of the cage.

Lesley and Christy then sat back, some distance away, anxiously waiting to see what would happen next.

Rocky looked out cautiously from his cage.

For the first time he could see without looking through the bars that separated him from the rest of the world. Shorty flew down and sat on top of the cage, talking with him all the time.

'It's okay Rocky,' she said 'they are letting you go. You know they bought you to set you free. So come on out and say hello to us all.' Rocky was feeling very nervous. It seemed a very big world out there, now that there was nothing between him and freedom. He hopped down onto the cage floor, walked to the edge of the open cage, and looked out fearfully.

'Are you sure this isn't a trick?' he asked Shorty. 'No, not at all.' Shorty replied. 'Here, I'll come in and say hello to show you.' And Shorty did just that. She flew into Rocky's cage and perched on the rung with him.

After awhile, Shorty told Rocky it was time to meet all the rest of the Ballinger gang. Rocky just nodded and, with a slight hesitation, hopped out of the cage onto the verandah. He looked up at the yellow bloodwood tree with all the other birds perched on the branches, watching.

This was always a big moment for the gang of escapees. Never though had an attempt at freeing a captive bird been this easy, and so gentle.

Shorty stood alongside Rocky, slowly starting to flap her wings and encouraging him to do the same. Next minute he found himself, ever so slowly, lifting into the air. Rocky took one quick look around at Lesley and Christy and, before he knew it, he was flying…. flying. That magical word he had only ever heard about – and now he knew what it truly meant!

Unlike Cherub's planned escape, Rocky's flight to freedom was very gentle and lovingly carried out. And the next minute he found himself perched in the branches of the tree with Shorty, Maxi, Cherub and the rest of the gang.

Lesley and Christy just looked at each other in awe as tears flowed gently down their faces. It had worked. The birds accepted Rocky and he had accepted them. He had flown free.

So many people had told them how cruel it would be to set a captive bird free. They were told a captive bird would not last long in the wild, as they did not have the skills to survive. People said other birds would attack them or it would simply starve as it would not know what plants and flowers to feed from, and eventually die a cruel death.

Lesley and Christy somehow knew that by hanging Rocky's cage on the verandah for the other birds to fly down to, eventually there would be some sort of bird-bonding happening and this would provide a flock for Rocky to join. And it had worked.

'So what are they doing now?' Cherub asked Shorty. 'It looks like they are filling up the seed and water bowls in the cage and hanging it back up, with one whole side left wide open. Why are they doing that?'

'I heard them talking before they set me free this morning' Rocky said suddenly. These were the first words he had spoken since he had experienced his miraculous flight to the tree. 'They wanted to make sure I had somewhere to fly back to, just in case'.

'Just in case what?' asked Cherub.

'In case I wasn't sure about where to get food and water from or if I needed somewhere to feel safe to sleep'. Rocky replied.

All the birds looked at each other, then down to the two women standing on the verandah looking up at them. And again Cherub heard her mother's words, and wondered at the possibility of humans and animals being able to live together in respect of each other's birthrights.

Over the next few weeks Rocky and Shorty did fly down and feed from the cage, sitting on the perch looking out at the world. And it wasn't long before they decided to become a pair of 'love birds'.

ONE YEAR LATER

The following summer Lesley was on the verandah late one afternoon and excitedly called to Christy to come out quickly.

'Look up there' she said, 'isn't that Rocky and Shorty?' Christy looked to where Lesley was pointing. Sure enough, there was the tell tale mark around Shorty's leg, of the chain she once wore and the slight chip in the side of Rocky's beak that always identified him. And sitting beside them were three little short-billed Corella baby birds.

Christy simply watched with her mouth opened in awe, shaking her head from side to side in wonder.

'Do you think they deliberately flew back to show us their family?' Lesley asked Christy, with tears in her eyes and an enormous smile on her face.

Christy looked from Lesley back to the tree, and could only nod her head in reply, still marvelling at what she saw.

Rocky and Shorty looked down at them. 'Do you think they know it is us and that we have come back to thank them for all they have done?' Shorty asked.

'Yes' Rocky replied. 'This was their dream. To free me so I could live the life I was born to live. They knew I was born to fly, and now they know that I have survived and brought new birds into the world, birds that were born into freedom.'

Cherub was perched in a branch with Maxi Ballinger, higher in the yellow bloodwood. She watched the birds and the people, and she knew she had only just begun to fulfill her destiny.

Over the past year Cherub had flown with the gang, learning all manner of skills. She had also travelled to many places, seeing all sorts of birds and animals in hideous forms of captivity and imprisonment.

She often felt her challenge to free them from their pain seemed enormous and out of reach. As she now looked down at the two women's happy, tear stained faces however, she knew there were enough people in the world who understood what she was trying to accomplish, and would be playing their part in the great tapestry of life. Cherub also now knew with absolute certainty that her task to bring love and enlightenment to all two legged, four pawed, winged and finned beings could and would happen.

And so, as the sun began to set on this wondrous moment, beyond that huge yellow bloodwood tree, in this most magical garden full of beautiful flowering plants and shrubs, the adventures of Cherub, the Rainbow Lorikeet, were truly only just beginning.

AUTHORS NOTE AND CHERUB'S FUTURE JOURNEYS

The stories of how Maxi Ballinger, a long-billed Corella, and Rocky, a short-billed Corella, were bought and ultimately obtained their freedom are both true. As is the coming together of Rocky and Shorty, and their subsequent return a year later with their new family.

I changed our names simply to allow fact and fiction to blend. At the end of the day though – it is based on a true story even though some of the animals and their interaction have obviously been imagined.

Lesley and I did, over a number of years, develop an amazingly beautiful garden, in the backyard of her home in Noosa, (Queensland, Australia,) where birds of many species flocked together.

Little did I know all those years back, that these stories and photos would eventually become **'Born to Fly.'**

It wasn't till I returned to Sydney for a few months in 1994, sharing with friends in a house in Hunters Hill, did the story start to write itself. One of the women had been given a Rainbow Lorikeet named Cherub as a gift, and was very upset at having a young bird living in a small cage on its own.

Each day while I was there, other lorikeets flew down to Cherub's cage and chirped with her.

My frustration at Cherub's owner not listening to me about Rocky and Shorty's happy story, and releasing Cherub to live with the flock of Lorikeets she was bonding with; was the catalyst for writing **'Born To Fly.'**

While it may be viewed as a children's book it is also an educational story for all ages. Many captive birds can and are being released back into nature safely and lovingly by many other caring people.

This is not the end of Cherub and her friends. Cherub will have many more adventures, which will be shared in subsequent books until we, as a species, understand we are caretakers and guardians of nature. Our role is to observe and delight in the many wondrous examples of nature and to teach each and every one of our children this precious gift, so we can all, truly, fly free.

And the real Cherub?

A few months after I returned to Queensland, I heard that Cherubs cage had been found on the ground with the door wide open. I choose to believe she had flown free with her flock.

ABOUT THE AUTHOR

Robyn's personal journey to become a published author began in May 1984, when she left her advertising career and the associated material benefits that defined her life at the time.
There is a saying that 'when we take the first step – we are given the next nine'.

When Robyn took that first step of leaving behind financial security, she had no idea how or where the next step would take her. All she knew was three things: she wanted to write; to discover more of who she was; and to make a positive difference in the world.

This 'deeply-felt' inner calling seemed to have a mind of its own, and through another series of events, Robyn found herself moving to Queensland's Sunshine Coast, in November 1984.

This move saw Robyn discovering a new field of communication where she began gaining the skills to assist others to free themselves from the limitations of their own thoughts and emotions.

2013 – ROBYN'S UPDATE

Fast forward to May 2013 - 29 years later. I have been living back in Sydney since September 1997. My work has branched out into a number of fields which includes creating and facilitating Team Development Programs for both business and community organisations.

I have also been privileged to produce and present a conversational style TV program, featuring Australian and International guests who are leaders in their fields of mind/body science, spirituality, and sustainability.

'They say we teach what we need to learn... and as we learn we teach.' I feel very blessed for I am finally learning to fly free in my own life while making a difference through doing what I love...and so it is time for this book to go out into the world.'

Another well known saying **'it is the journey not the destination that matters in the end'** has often popped into my mind over the past 29 years, especially when obstacles seemed insurmountable and I felt riddled with self-doubt at the choices I was making (and I am sure many of you know what I am talking about here in regard to your own life journey)

What I have come to know is this 'it is the balance of what I receive...and what I give...on a daily basis...that defines my own level of inner happiness and contentment'.

I am now also a budding Elder who is becoming more conscious in stepping forward...and I look ahead to the next 29 years of my life and the cumulative lives of us all...and wonder what 2042 will bring.

That does seem such a long way off...and yet when I look back to when this chapter of my life began in 1984.....it went so fast!

Which brings me to a question that I hear people asking more and more . . . **'How can I make a positive contribution?'**

One solution is that sometimes the simple act of educating ourselves to become more consciously aware of possibilities and potentials is one of the greatest gifts we can offer the world. Because from this point all things are possible!

SEVEN GENERATION SUSTAINABILITY

One area of self-education could include understanding and actualising an ecological concept called **'Seven Generation Sustainability'** - which urges the current generation of humans to live sustainably and work for the benefit of the seventh generation into the future.

This concept is common to most indigenous peoples on our planet. I first heard it in relation to the Hopi Indians. It is about thinking and planning 'seven generations' ahead (140 years into the future) and deciding whether the decisions we make today, will benefit children seven generations into the future.

So in looking forward to the next 29 years of my life (and the year 2042) it may seem a long way off...in reality it is less than two generations ahead...which is a very short time compared to the suggested 140 years.

I choose to believe that over the next generation or two, we will all begin to heal our hearts and in turn free many people, birds and animals from a life of captivity and suffering to a life full of love, freedom and wonderment...for we are all caretakers of this wondrous planet Earth and we were all born to fly free.

Take care
Robyn Walker

HONOUR OTHERS AS GEESE DO

Next time you see geese heading south for the winter, flying along in a 'V' formation, you might consider what science has discovered as to why they fly that way......

As each bird flaps its wings, it creates an uplift for the bird immediately following. By flying in 'V' formation, the whole flock adds 71 percent greater flying range than if each bird flew on it's own.

People who share a common direction and sense of community can better get where they are going more quickly and easily because they are travelling on the thrust of one another.

When a goose falls out of formation, it suddenly feels the drag and resistance of trying to go it alone....and quickly gets back in formation to take advantage of the "lifting power"

If we have as much sense as a goose, we will stay in formation with those that are heading in the same direction as we are (and willing to accept their help as well as give ours to others)

When a lead goose gets tired, it rotates back into the formation and another goose flies point. It is sensible to take turns doing demanding jobs. With people, as with geese, we are interdependent on each other.

Geese honk from behind to encourage those up front to keep up their speed. We need to make sure our honking from behind is encouraging and not something else.

Finally, and this is important, when a goose gets sick, or is wounded by gunshots and falls out of formation, two other geese fall out with that goose and follow it down

to lend help and protection. They stay with that fallen goose until it is able to fly again or dies.

Only then, do they launch out on their own, or with another formation, to catch up with their group.

If we have the sense of a goose, we will stand by each other in difficult times, as when we are strong.

Milton Olson

'THE CIRCLE OF LIFE'

CHIEF WHITE CLOUD

Mankind has a poor understanding of life. He mistakes knowledge for wisdom. He tries to unveil the holy secrets of our father, the Great Spirit.

He attempts to impose his laws and ways on Mother Earth. Even though he, himself, is part of nature, he chooses to disregard and ignore it for the sake of his own immediate gain.

But the laws of nature are far stronger than those of mankind.

Man must awake at last, and learn to understand how little time there remains before he will become the cause of his own downfall. And he has so much to learn. To learn to see with the heart.

He must learn to respect Mother Earth - She who has given life to everything; to our brothers and sisters, the animals and plants; to the rivers, the lakes, the oceans and the winds.

He must realize that this planet does not belong to him, but that he has to care for and maintain the delicate balance of nature for the sake of the wellbeing for our children and all future generations.

It is the duty of mankind to preserve the earth and the creation of the Great Spirit.

Mankind being but a grain of sand in the Holy Circle which encloses all of life.

www.ingramcontent.com/pod-product-compliance
Lightning Source LLC
Chambersburg PA
CBHW060821290526

45792CB00005BB/1755